SIMPLE BUT COMPLICATED

SANIA TABASSUM M A

Dedication:

With love for the ones who were left out,
with hugs for the ones who were left cold,
with words for the ones who were left unheard.
You are seen. You are felt. You are not alone.

Contents

Contents

Preface

It's just a book filled with poems full of emotions we all go through at some point of time in life.

Acknowledgements

Special Thanks

To my **late brother - Roshan**, who believed in my words even when I doubted them—your support still echoes in my heart.

To my **mother**, whose strength is endless, whose hands never knew rest, and whose love, though unspoken, shaped me.

To **Kim Seokjin, Min Yoongi, Jung Hoseok, Kim Namjoon, Park Jimin, Kim Taehyun & Jeon Jungkook** - Legit Angels who have helped countless people become a better version of themselves.

And to the few souls who stood by me—your presence was a light in my darkest moments. Thank you.

1. Me? Disposable.

They smiled, they laughed, they held my hand,
spoke in whispers, called me *friend*.
But love was just a game to play,
and I was never meant to stay.
I was the shoulder, the listening ear,
the keeper of secrets, the catcher of tears.
But when the storms had cleared away,
they left—like I was yesterday.
I gave, they took, I bled, they fed,
left me hollow, left me dead.
Their words, like honey, sweet but thin,
coated lies I let sink in.
Now my name is just a ghost,
a number lost, a past they toast.
And I wonder, was I blind,
or were they fake this whole damn time?

2. The Man who calls himself a Father

He speaks, and the walls shrink inward,
his voice—a storm, a fist, a weight.
I learned young how silence breaks,
how love can wear the mask of hate.
Hands should build, hands should mend,
but his only knew how to bruise.
Pain became my mother tongue,
fear, the lullaby I never chose.
I stopped flinching, stopped fighting,
let the words sink deep like rust.
If I don't feel it, it doesn't hurt—
if I don't cry, then I am tough.
But at night, when the world is quiet,
I touch the scars he'll never see.
And I wonder—if a father destroys you,
is he still family?

3. Silent Screams

The walls have heard the cries I swallowed,
the floor has felt the weight of my fall.
Bruises bloom like quiet confessions,
hidden beneath sleeves too long, too tall.
I have mastered the art of silence,
smiling through shattered bones.
They ask, *"Are you okay?"* and I nod,
because pain is best endured alone.
But tonight, I write my story in scars,
not for pity, not for shame—
but for the ones still locked in whispers,
afraid to speak their pain.
No more hiding in the shadows,
no more suffering in disguise.
This voice was caged for far too long—
tonight, it finally **flies.**

4. The Mother I Miss

She wakes before the sun can rise,
hands worn, heart heavy, tired eyes.
The world demands, and she obeys,
working through the endless days.
I watch her moving, swift and cold,
a woman built from steel and gold.
Once, her laughter filled our home,
now it's silence—I feel alone.
Her hands once braided strands of mine,
now they only count the time.
Her voice once soft, now edged with weight,
burdened by the life she chases late.
I know she loves me—still, I ache,
for the warmth that time and toil take.
She built my world, but lost her place,
a mother's love I barely trace.
And I wonder, if she ever sees,
the girl still waiting—just to be seen.

5. Shattered Blueprints

They gave me a map, traced in bold,
Lines of duty, paths of gold.
"Follow," they said, "this is your way,"
But what of my dreams, left to decay?
I built my hopes with glass so fine,
Fragile, yet stubborn—aching to shine.
But glass can break with the weight of doubt,
And their voices crushed what I dreamed about.
Each step I take, I walk on shards,
Bleeding out under their guards.
Yet they tell me, "This is the path you must go,"
Ignoring the scars that silently show.
What if my dreams were never theirs?
What if I dared? What if I cared?
But I keep building, though trembling inside,
Hiding my wounds, swallowing pride.
Maybe one day, I'll carve my own way,
A castle of glass that won't betray.
And if it shatters, if it falls apart,
At least it was mine—my work of art.

6. A Battle No One Sees

I wake up wearing the same old mask,
a painted smile, a hollow laugh.
No one sees the war inside,
the weight I carry, the wounds I hide.
The world demands, *"Stay strong, hold on,"*
but never asks, *"How long can you?"*
Each breath feels borrowed, each step too heavy,
as if the air itself disapproves.
I whisper, *"Maybe tomorrow,"*
but tomorrow never hears.
The darkness calls in gentle tones,
promising rest, stealing years.
But some small part of me still fights,
still holds a flicker in the night.
Perhaps not for love, perhaps not for hope—
but for the chance to heal **one more time.**

7. Life After Death

She whispered her goodbyes in the dead of night,

Tracing farewells on fogged-up glass.

A heart too heavy, a mind too loud,

She swore this breath would be her last.

Her father's fists had carved deep scars,

Not on her skin, but in her soul.

Her mother's eyes, so cold, so sharp,

Made her feel like she'd never be whole.

They called her *a curse, a mistake, an abomination,*

A shadow unworthy of light.

Fake friends laughed with honeyed tongues,

But left when the world turned quiet.

She had nothing, no arms to run to,

No voice to scream, no place to hide.

She was drowning, lost, a name unloved—

A ghost while still alive.

But the dawn didn't wait for her sorrow to win,

It pulled her back with burning light.

Soft embers flickered in hollow ribs,

Whispering, *Not yet. Not tonight.*

So she rose—

Not like the girl they broke apart,

But as something fierce, untamed, alive.

Not a ghost, not a shadow, not just a name—

A phoenix with fire in her eyes.

She was never the weak one.
She was never the curse.
She was *life itself*, reborn from the ashes,
And now—she burns.

8. Restless Rest

They say my bed must be my comfort,
a place where dreams should softly land.
But they don't know the wars I fight,
while lying still with trembling hands.
The pillows cradle weary bones,
yet never hold the weight I bear.
Sheets wrap around my hollow frame,
but never warm the cold despair.
They call me lazy, call me weak,
mock the hours that slip away.
But they don't see the endless nights,
where sleep and peace refuse to stay.
My eyes stay open, lost in thought,
a prisoner in my weary skin.
The world moves fast, but I stand still,
too tired to lose, too weak to win.
Morning comes—I rise once more,
another mask, another day.
But this bed knows the truth I hide,
I rest, yet never drift away.

9. Playing Along

I wake up, I smile, I play my role,
A picture of calm, in perfect control.
They see the laughter, the charm, the grace,
But never the war I silently face.
They say, "You're strong," they say, "You shine,"
Yet no one hears the screams in my mind.
The weight of the past, the ghosts of my pain,
Press on my chest, but I don't complain.
I move through the crowd, unseen, unheard,
My lips speak peace, my heart slurs words.
If they looked closer, if they saw through,
Would they still love me, if they knew?
But I am the secret, the unspoken ache,
A beautiful mask, too flawless to break.
And so, I'll keep smiling, I'll keep playing along,
Even when I no longer feel like I belong.

10. Roots beneath the Strains

We live in the quiet hum of hard work,
hands worn from effort,
eyes tired but never defeated,
finding peace in the simplest of moments.
There's no gold to count,
no luxury to chase—
but our hearts beat rich,
wrapped in laughter, warmth, and struggle.
The house may be small,
but love fills every corner,
and in every tired step,
there's pride in the rise after every fall.
We don't need much,
just enough to breathe and share,
finding beauty in the dirt on our shoes,
the sweat on our brow,
the joy in the simplicity of simply living.

11. The Loner's canvas

In the silence, I paint my scars,
each line a scream,
each color a confession—
pain spilled across the canvas,
no words to mute its truth.
Shadows rise like ghosts,
tangled in the black,
while reds bleed into the white,
fury crashing against calm—
and all I do is watch,
my soul unraveling in brushstrokes.
There is no audience here,
only the weight of my own heart,
struggling to exist on this blank,
empty, unforgiving space.
I paint the broken parts of me
that no one else dares to see,
capturing my wounds in a form
too painful for the world,
but perfect for the one
who understands this kind of loneliness.

12. Draped in Midnight

"Are you always funeral ready?" they tease,
as if black were a mourning plea.
But to me, it's more than grief or loss,
it's the only shade that doesn't lie to me.
It doesn't scream, it doesn't beg,
it doesn't pretend to shine too bright.
It wraps around like a quiet shield,
a color that finally **feels right.**
They call it dark, they call it dull,
but I call it *home*—soft and full.
A whisper of comfort, a shadowed embrace,
in black, I don't have to explain my place.
So let them wonder, let them stare,
let them think I'm drowning in despair.
But black is not a wound, nor a goodbye—
it's just the color where **I feel alive.**

13. Brother, You are just away for a while right?

I set the table like I always do,
two plates, two cups—one chair left askew.
My hands hesitate, my chest caves in,
but I place it anyway, like you'll walk in.
They say you're gone, but I don't hear.
Your voice still lingers, painfully clear.
Your laughter hums in the walls at night,
but the silence cuts deeper in morning light.
I talk to you in whispers low,
pretend you answer, pretend you know.
But the air is heavy, hollow, cruel—
a house filled with memories, but never *you*.
They tell me, *accept it, let it be,*
but how do I grieve what still breathes in me?
How do I let go when my heart still waits,
listening for footsteps that never break?
You're just away—just far, not dead.
Not ashes, not silence, not words unsaid.
You'll walk in soon, I swear it's true…
because this world is unbearable—
without you.

14. Let me Embrace You for a while

If you're reading this with trembling hands,
If your heart feels like a home abandoned,
If the weight of your thoughts is louder than love—
Then let these words hold you for a while.
You are *not* a lost cause.
You are not too broken to be understood,
Not too damaged to be loved.
You are not the burden they made you believe you are.
I know the nights feel longer than your will to stay,
And silence echoes louder than a scream.
But somewhere in the darkness,
Even the smallest spark is still fire.
You are that fire.
Even when you're tired.
Even when you doubt it.
Even when you can't see the light in yourself—
I promise, it's still there.
Rest here for a moment.
Breathe.
Let these words wrap around you like a warmth you forgot existed.
You are not alone.
You never were.
And even if no one has told you today—
I'm proud of you for being here.

For holding on.
For still believing, even just a little bit,
That you are meant to be.
Because you are.

15. Hey, Moon… Wassup?

The world sleeps, but I stay awake,
resting my soul beneath your silver gaze.
Tell me, dear Moon, how many hearts
have spilled their secrets into your light?
Do you hear the whispered apologies
never spoken to the ones who left?
The silent screams of souls too tired to fight,
too broken to believe in another dawn?
Do you carry the weight of unshed tears,
collect them like raindrops in your glow?
Do you know the names of those who
only feel seen when you shine?
Some beg for lost love to return,
some curse the stars for their cruel fate,
some wish to disappear within your light—
a longing to be weightless, to be free.
And then, there are those like me—
who ask for nothing,
who simply sit in your quiet glow,
knowing you will listen,
knowing you will stay.
Tell me, dear Moon,
how many hearts have you held tonight?
And if I am just another—
will you hold mine too?

16. Seven Souls, One Light

Seven voices, echoing through the dark,
reaching places they'll never see.
A lifeline woven from melodies,
saving souls like mine—silently.
They do not know my name, my face,
yet their words have built my home.
Each note, a whisper: *"Hold on, stay."*
Each lyric, a reason not to feel alone.
They never saw the nights I cried,
or the way their songs held me tight.
Yet somehow, they pulled me back to life,
turning my storms into softer skies.
So here I stand, heart in my hands,
whispering thanks they'll never hear.
Seven souls, a light so vast—
guiding me through every fear.
They may never know I exist,
but I will love them just the same.
For in a world that tried to break me,
they were the ones who let me stay.

17. Take it or Leave it

• 19 •

I am who I am,

no filters, no lies,

no need to explain myself

to anyone who can't see the truth in my eyes.

I don't apologize for my fire,

for my chaos,

for the noise I make

when the world wants silence.

I wear my flaws like a crown,

and my scars like art—

because each piece of me

was earned, not given.

I stopped seeking permission

to exist, to speak, to breathe—

I stopped pretending to be anything

other than unapologetically me.

So take it or leave it,

I'm not here to impress,

I'm here to be real,

to live loud,

to love myself

in ways the world refuses to understand.

18. Purple walls, endless visions

The walls stand bare,

waiting for a voice,

a hue to transform them,

to fill the emptiness

with whispers of imagination.

Purple calls to me,

deep and rich,

a shade of dreams and mystery,

the perfect canvas for my thoughts

to stretch out and roam free.

Each stroke of color,

a brush with freedom,

a touch of chaos,

a burst of peace—

the room breathes with the rhythm of my soul,

shaped by my vision,

built for my mind to wander.

I see it now—

a space, not just to exist,

but to create, to dream,

to live in the midst of color and comfort,

where every corner holds a story,

and the walls whisper the secrets of my heart.

19. Emails and Stuff

The clock blinks, the emails pile,
another day lost to deadlines,
chasing a finish line
that only moves further away.
They say work is survival,
but what is a life
where the soul is starving,
where dreams gather dust on a desk?
So I learn—
to step away, to breathe,
to give my time not just to labor,
but to laughter, to love, to me.
Because in the end,
no title, no paycheck, no applause
will matter more than this:
the life I built for myself,
not just the work I did for others.

20. Humbled by Heights

I stood before the mountains,
chest high, chin raised,
believing I had conquered enough,
believing I had seen it all.
But the peaks laughed in silence,
whispering truths the wind carried—
that strength is not in standing tall,
but in knowing how small you are.
With every step, my pride cracked,
crumbling like loose gravel beneath me,
teaching me that beauty isn't owned,
only witnessed, only felt.
At the summit, breathless, undone,
I found not victory, but wonder—
a world too vast to be tamed,
a heart too small to contain it all.

21. Ink & Ache

They ask why I do it,
why I let the needle kiss my skin,
why I trade blood for art,
why pain feels like home.
The sting—it hums, it sings,
a melody of quiet suffering,
of battles fought beneath my ribs,
of wounds too deep for eyes to see.
Each line, each shade,
is a scream I never spoke,
a scar I chose,
a story I own.
They see colors,
I feel release.
They call it beauty,
I call it survival.

22. Bloom & Breathe

Beneath a sky brushed in pastels,
cherry blossoms whisper in the wind,
soft as sighs, fleeting as time—
a quiet promise that beauty is not meant to last.
Petals fall like unfinished thoughts,
landing on open palms,
only to slip away—
a reminder that nothing truly belongs to us.
Yet, in their short-lived grace,
there is no sorrow, no fear—
only the gentle surrender
to the rhythm of life, to the art of letting go.
I sit beneath their fading blush,
breathing in the silence they leave behind,
and for the first time,
peace feels like something I can hold.

23. My Own Song

The beat starts low,
but it vibrates through my soul,
a pulse that's mine,
no one else's,
no rules to follow,
just the rhythm of my truth.
I lose myself in every note,
the melody a reflection of my mind—
wild, untamed,
dancing between silence and sound,
where I am both the music and the listener,
the composer and the song.
There are no boundaries here,
no "should" or "must"
only freedom—
the kind that rises from within,
from the deep places
where words fall short.
In this space, I am free—
to speak, to scream, to be,
unfiltered, unchained,
living my own anthem,
playing the soundtrack to my own world.

24. Passing Strangers Lasting Self

They came like seasons,
some with the warmth of summer,
some with the chill of winter,
none meant to stay forever.
I held on too tightly,
aching at every goodbye,
forgetting that even fallen leaves
find their way back to the earth.
People go, hearts shift,
promises fade like old echoes—
but I remain,
whole in my own embrace.
I have learned:
the only love that never leaves
is the one I give myself.

25. Love? Oh, It rained that day

The sky weeps,

and so do I—

drops fall like whispers,

touching my skin,

and something in me stirs,

soft and unspoken.

You appear through the mist,

eyes caught by mine

as if the storm had brought us here,

together, in this moment

where the world fades

and only our hearts remain.

The rain becomes a symphony,

each drop a note we play,

slow, gentle,

the rhythm of love blooming in silence.

I never believed in love at first sight—

but then you looked at me,

and the rain wasn't the only thing falling.

26. The Roads we took

It wasn't the love I held on to,
not the touch, not the whispered name.
But the wind in my hair, the sky stretched wide,
the freedom that set my soul aflame.
We chased the sun through winding trails,
danced with shadows on mountain peaks.
Laughter spilled like rivers wild,
words unspoken, yet hearts would speak.
The wheels spun stories into dust,
each mile a memory etched in gold.
Not of him—but of the journey,
the hills that made me brave and bold.
Now the roads still call my name,
but the footsteps beside me are gone.
I don't miss the man—I miss the journey,
the wild, the free, the moving on.

27. Approval, It seems!!!

I walk their path,
step by step,
to the rhythm of their expectations—
always rushing, always chasing,
but never really moving.
They say who I should be,
how I should smile,
what I should say,
and I wonder,
when will I get to breathe for me?
Every choice, every decision,
is weighed against their gaze,
like a shadow that won't leave,
like a mirror reflecting someone I never wanted to be.
I'm screaming inside,
but all they hear is silence,
as I keep running their race,
but my soul—
it's stuck, waiting,
aching for the chance to live for itself.

28. Emotions

Let emotions flow in at times,

maybe at hard times or rough phases—

just let it flow.

The more you hold it in,

the more you end up being hurt.

Keep the heart at ease, as it is too delicate.

Your soul longs for the embrace of your own self.

Life gets easier, step by step—

but only when you don't push yourself too hard.

It's okay to take a break.

But when you come back, ensure

that you are your best self

and give yourself your best.

Keep loving yourself for who you are today.

Also, if you need to hear this—

"I am proud of you,"

even at your most vulnerable time.

So, just let your emotions flow.

29. Inner Conflicts

• 31 •

At times, when I am on my own—
oh wait, I am always on my own.
Okay, so since I'm always on my own,
I think of things that could possibly happen.
Would they be good, or would they be bad?
But then I think—
Am I good enough for good things to happen to me?
Or am I so bad that only bad things will happen to me?
All these thoughts keep rushing into my mind every now and then.
I sit helpless, staring at nothing,
all blank about where life has been taking me.
I also wonder where I am taking myself
in the life I have been living.
Then I just push away all these thoughts
to the back of my head
and continue breathing—
something I had briefly stopped while I sat to think,
Okay, Now I am back to reality relieving myself from the Inner Conflicts

30. Masking a Smile – Art

Sitting in a room full of lively, lovely people,
I still somehow manage to hear the noise of the void in my heart.
Everything screams *perfect*, and everyone seems happy.
But my mind screams—there's nothing that is perfect,
and there is no one that's always happy.
But what do I do? Well, I guess I shall just blend in.
Flash a smile of pretense that might possibly
hide the emptiness in my eyes.
Let's focus on the best and ignore the rest,
because life shall continue to put you to the test.
Come on now, let's gear up and behave—
grown up, being one smiley face among all the others.
Among all of those who hide their sorrows perfectly,
with that beautiful mask of the smile on their face.

31. Running? Yeah, Running

What are we up to?

No idea, right?

I guess we are all just running—

sometimes from people,

sometimes from ourselves,

mostly in an invisible race,

sometimes from a truth that hurts.

We all talk about *work*.

But then, we tend to forget and continue running.

Aimless, we keep trying to reach some aim.

But what is that aim? We don't know.

All we need sometimes is just a break,

but we are afraid of stopping.

Hence, we keep running.

And when we see others way ahead of us,

we tend to give up because we feel

that we have been running yet not moving in any direction.

But still, we pick up ourselves,

control our thoughts,

and then continue running.

32. Let's Slow Dance in Rain

Holding each other close,

Close enough to hear a loud heartbeat,

But far enough to look into each other's eyes—

The eyes that hold entire galaxies.

Let me feel your hands on my waist, the gift of touch,

A touch strong enough to make me melt,

But not enough to slip into lust.

Let me just capture this moment of ours—

Beautiful enough to cherish forever,

But not enough to mark a date,

For this will be the sweetest moment of our lives.

Let's just live in this pure stillness,

With love deep enough to feel loved,

But not enough to declare it aloud.

Some love is meant to last for eternity.

Let's slow dance in the rain,

Drenched enough to make the cold disappear,

But not enough to soak our souls.

Let's slow dance in the rain on a cliff top,

The moon shining bright enough to hold back the dark,

But not enough for us to read its glow—

That light is already in our hearts.

Come now, my love, I've given enough reasons,

But not enough to take your heart as my gain.

For now, let's just slow dance in the rain.

33. Untold

Do you remember how we met?

We fought over something silly—I cried, and you left.

Then we talked it out and became friends.

From that moment on, we kept talking, meeting, and being together,

like it was meant to be.

You stayed when everyone else walked away.

You held me when I was broken.

You made me feel alive, even when my family didn't care.

You made me feel strong and helped me trust myself again.

You are the reason I believe angels still exist.

You kept every promise you made.

You always made sure I was okay.

The songs we sing for each other,

The feelings we share,

Let's keep this unnamed relationship forever,

Because it means the world to me.

You are unique and so special to me.

I don't even remember my first wish,

But my last wish is to have you with me forever.

34. Listen - I Love You.

You are the masterpiece I will never be able to paint with my love,
The poem my heart feels, but my pen will never be able to write.
The story I know by heart,
Yet my lips will never be able to tell.
A memory so beautiful, my mind will never be able to forget.
And let me tell you something about me—
I am that girl who will never be able to love anyone the way I loved you.

35. I Am Afraid

I am afraid that everything will disappear.

I am afraid that you will walk away & everything else will too.

I am afraid that you will forget me and with that, my existence will end.

I am afraid that you will see me as a stranger & everything about me will become strange to myself too.

I am afraid that you will hate me & I shall cease to believe in love—if it's you who will tell me to leave.

I am afraid to believe that you are mine because I know I can't belong to you.

I am afraid of all these voices in my head that tell me that I will hurt you.

How will I ever hurt you, when it will be me who feels your pain?

I am just afraid of everything now—'cause even I am scared to lose you, as you are my everything.

36. For who You Are

Yes, yes, you—what have you done to my soul?
It yearns for you.
Hey, just your eyes—why do I feel drunk
when your gaze meets mine?
Look, it's not easy, not easy at all
to keep my heart stable when you are around.
Babe, can you just not? Can you just not treat me so well?
I don't deserve this much care.
Damn, I am just so done with myself,
but still, you keep giving me all your love.
Why? Why do you have to be like this?
You say that I am worth everything
when I feel so worthless.
Okay, I'll just trust you. I'll lean on you
and let things happen. I'll trust you
for the person **you are.**

37. Together?

If only I could tell you what I feel,

I bet your heart would cry for me.

The way I toss around in my bed at night,

crying and begging God just to get some sleep.

I've been pretending to be the strongest soldier out there,

but deep inside, I know I'm running out of weapons.

Could you just hold me close to your heart

and let me feel the warmth again?

Could you just let me hold your hand

in my cold ones again?

"Why?" Is that what you want to ask?

No, please don't—because I don't have an answer for that.

Didn't you say our love felt like a fairy tale?

I guess you were right when you said so,

but not every ship that leaves the shore always sails.

What we are now is exactly the opposite

of what we wanted to be—together.

Now, I finally realize that we were never

meant to be together.

38. You? Home?

I was drunk,
but still, my body carries your scent instead of the stench of alcohol.
What have you done to me?
Why am I getting so delusional?
Should I blame the alcohol,
or do I blame you for being the reason my heart beats so fast?
I am tired of running away.
For once—just once—should I run into your arms and call it home?
The home where I belong, the home that gives me rest.

39. Her

She was like fire;

her eyes held all the fierceness.

She stood all by herself.

But then, she was like water too.

She spread prosperity everywhere she went,

moulding herself into every vessel she was poured into.

If she was like water, then what made her turn into fire?

Let me tell you—

they took and took until she was empty.

But people never stopped expecting from her.

When she stopped giving, they called her names.

She was left all alone in pain,

isolated and cast aside.

Now, she saw their true faces.

And then, she decided—enough was enough.

"I will stop giving and destroy those who hurt me.

They shall burn in my fire.

Now, I will be that fire."

40. Aren't we Making Love?

• 42 •

We reached our bedroom, and I closed the door behind us.

I turned around only to look straight into your eyes.

They are talking—I know that language.

Just look into my eyes, see, watch them respond to yours.

You came closer; my breath hitched.

In no time, I was pinned to the same door I looked at just minutes ago.

Now, I feel your breath on my lips. Stop with the teasing and let me taste them already.

I never realized when you stripped me of my clothes, and we landed on the bed.

But wait—

Didn't I want to be stopped?

Or, truthfully, did my soul want to be stopped?

Okay, let me just look into those eyes again.

Oh, shit.

No, no, we aren't making love.

We are just having sex.

What did I even think of? But still, it's okay.

If I make love to you, aren't we making love?

41. What was I even thinking?

I saw him at a distance, standing there with his earphones on, head bobbing. Maybe he was listening to some rock music?

I can be wrong, though. Oh, damn! Oops.

Did he just look at me? Forget it—it was just a glance. Maybe he just looked elsewhere.

But wait! What if he *did* look at me?

Silly me, I am smiling like an idiot.

Shouldn't I stop looking at him?

Nah, it's alright. It's not like there's anything to admire.

I was wrong. I was *totally* wrong.

The more I looked at him, the more I was falling for him.

I was stupid enough not to even realize it.

So what? So what if I fell for him at first sight?

It wouldn't take much to move on from a man I didn't even talk to.

I was naïve, for it was not admiration, not attraction, not lust.

It was *love*.

Love at first sight. *Hah!*

I know. What was I even thinking while looking at him?

42. Until You Found Me

I believed I would never find true love—
A love that could hold me together,
A love that defied all negativity in my mind,
A love that would take away my insecurities,
A love that would help me overcome my latent fears.
But then you came into my life—
With eyes in which I drowned myself,
A cute nose that I love to boop,
Fluffy cheeks that remind me of the flowers in spring,
Lips that glow, always, like the golden hues of my favorite flowers.
That boxy smile feels like a Christmas present
Left for me under a Christmas tree.
To what do I owe this pleasure and happiness of longing to be found
by you?
Yes, I say—it's not me who found you,
But *you* who found me.
And now, my life is full of joy.
Because I know how bad it was—until *you found me*.

43. Is it possible for you to Love me?

Sometimes, I just sit by the windowsill,

Looking at the sky and thinking about you.

Why are you just so perfect to be true?

Life seems to have taken a new turn because of you.

I don't know what I will do without you now.

I have forgotten me and only remember you.

Is it my heartbeat, or your smile that makes me feel this way?

Like I am flying in the sky,

I don't feel my feet anymore.

Has it always been like this for you, or have you made me anew?

I haven't been this happy before.

Why am I scared to love you?

Why do I think that you are too rare, too amazing?

Why does my heart smile just at the thought of you?

I am afraid I will hurt you, but tears don't feel hurt anymore.

I know that I love you, but will you ever love me the way I love you?

Will you ever love me?

44. What If? But,

What if I found the person who loves me for me?
But again, am I worth being loved?
What if life becomes beautiful all of a sudden?
But again, don't I just deserve it to be bad?
What if the heavens finally heard my prayers?
But then, am I not the Satan that was disowned?
What if I finally wanted to live?
But then, eventually, wasn't I supposed to die?
What if everything seems to be falling into place?
But isn't what falls bound to be broken, shattered flat?
What if my better had now begun?
But doesn't every beginning have its end?
This way, I would just keep having conflicts with my own thoughts.
The constant fear of my *"what if"* turning into *"but."*

45. Just be there, For Once

Bringing oneself to a state of letting it all out can be a difficult task.

But when one does that, they are at their most vulnerable.

Just imagine the level of trust they have in you to let their guard down
and be themselves in front of you.

Shouldn't you be a little careful with their emotions and be
considerate?

All that they need is for you to listen.

They can tell themselves, *"It's okay, you'll be fine,"*

but what they need from you is probably a warm hug

or a pat on their shoulder for encouragement.

So, for once, just be there.

Listen to them, hold their hand, and just stay around.

The level of relief brought in silence is very important to them.

So instead of just saying, *"I'm there,"*

be there; Just be there, for once.

46. What do I Need?

He stood at the end of the hallway,

Stepped closer and closer until I realized I was pinned against the wall.

He was just eight inches apart from my face.

He looked straight into my eyes, but still,

He was staring at my soul.

Like he wanted to devour me, taste every bit of me, take me whole.

I felt him come closer again, and now,

I could feel his lips brushing on mine.

The sparkle on my lips—what did it do to me?

I was distracted by his voice,

Also perfectly feeling everything he was saying on my skin.

He said,

"You, my little princess, do not need kisses.

You need your soul to be sucked out through your mouth but still want to feel euphoric.

You do not just want hands all over you.

You need to feel every single inch in your soul,

And still be able to want more."

You do not need just another release, something that's normal.

You need to feel your legs tremble,

Your skin burning,

Your hair soaked in sweat,

Your body all painted and still not feel *painted*.

And then he stepped away from me to look at the piece of art he created—

The chaos he caused.

He smirked; I wanted to punch him in his face.

Although the more *I* wanted to do it,

All my heart & soul longed for

Was him—to be closer, so close

That I could be under his skin,

Only if that's the closest I could be to him.

Yeah, he is right.

All I need is him.

47. Will I Ever find True Love?

I have given my heart to hands too rough,
to souls too hollow, to lips that lied.
I have searched for warmth in frozen chests,
begging for love in a world turned blind.
I have traced my name in fading echoes,
in whispers meant for someone else.
I've stood beneath the moon at midnight,
asking why I'm always left by myself.
Is love a game I was never meant to win?
A cruel illusion meant to tease?
Or am I simply unworthy of belonging,
forever lost in love's disease?
I reach for souls, but they slip through,
like sand that never wished to stay.
Tell me, Moon, do I keep searching?
Or is love just not meant for me?

48. Lost Love

I trace the ghosts of yesterday,

where your laughter still lingers soft in the air.

The echoes whisper your name in the silence,

but you're not here—you're nowhere.

My hands still reach for a warmth long faded,

fingers curling around empty space.

The moonlight feels colder without you beside me,

its silver glow, a hollow embrace.

I pass by places that knew our story,

now strangers to the love we bled.

The bench where we carved forever in whispers

is just wood and memories instead.

You are not mine, not anymore,

yet my heart refuses to learn.

It still beats in the rhythm of missing,

still aches for the love that won't return.

Tell me, do you ever look back at us,

or has time been kinder to you?

For me, the past is an open wound—

one that still bleeds in shades of you.

49. Her Choices without Options

She sits at the edge of midnight,
where the silence is louder than words.
A tired girl with trembling hands,
tracing choices that already hurt.
The walls hum with echoes of voices,
sharp as glass, cold as stone.
They tell her who she should be,
but never ask what she wants to own.
She has carried their dreams like burdens,
folded herself to fit their mold.
Yet in their eyes, she's always lacking,
too quiet, too soft, too bold.
The weight of love feels like shackles,
a bond that bruises, never breaks.
How do you choose between yourself
and the family that makes your heart ache?
So she stares at the crossroad before her,
each path lined with sacrifice.
One leads to the girl they raised her to be,
the other—to the girl she's never met twice.
And she wonders, just for a moment,
if choosing herself means she's wrong.
Or if, maybe, for the first time ever—
she has been right all along.

50. Dear Reader,

This is the last ink you'll see from me,

A final breath from a heart that never learned to rest.

But don't mistake this for an end—

It's just a brief silence, a pause before the storm hits again.

I've bled my truth onto these pages,

Laid bare every tear, every scar.

You've walked through the fire with me,

Felt the heat, the burn, the war.

I won't thank you in the usual way,

With soft words or hollow praise.

No, my gratitude is louder than that—

It's in every line, every verse, every phrase.

You, who felt the ache of my soul,

You, who lived in the depth of these words—

I don't need to say much more,

Because you've already heard.

So let this be a promise, not a goodbye.

I'll return, stronger, fiercer, more broken than before.

You'll see me again, and I'll leave you breathless—

For there's so much more left to say, so much more to pour.

Thank you, for seeing me—

For witnessing my fight, my fall, my rise.

But know this, the end of this chapter is not the end,

Just the quiet before the next storm ignites.

9 7 9 8 8 9 7 4 4 7 4 0 4